Editor Lis Edwards
Consultant Paul Whalley
Designer Design Machine
Production Susan Mead

Acknowledgements

Graham Allen/Linden Artists Front cover, 16-17
20-21, 24-25, 28-29, 36-37
Rhoda Burns/Drawing Attention 12-13, 18-19,
22-23, 26-27, 34-35, 38-39
Hayward Art Group Back Cover
Pat Lenander/Temple Art Group 10-11
Tony Morris/Linda Rogers Associates 30-31
Charlotte Snook 8-9, 40-41
John Thompson-Steinkraus/John Martin and
Artists Limited 14-15, 32-33
Endpaper photograph D. & K. Urry/Bruce
Coleman Ltd

Front cover: Blue tits and a coal tit feeding on
a bag of nuts in a town garden.
Endpapers: Black-headed and herring gulls at
their roost on a London reservoir.

Macdonald Educational Ltd
Holywell House
Worship Street
London EC2A 2EN

Printed in Hong Kong

ISBN 0 356 07120 0

WILDLIFE IN TOWNS

Graham Carter

Macdonald Educational

Contents

All about towns

Looking for wildlife

Towns and cities are often thought of as hostile places, where plants and animals have to struggle to survive among the concrete, noise and dirt. In fact they are full of wildlife, though you may have to look hard for some of it.

Everyone who lives in a town is surrounded by other living things. Some of these animals and plants are easy to find. Trees grow in city parks, gardens and even in holes cut out of pavements. Birds are everywhere; in gardens, on rooftops, in trees and in the city street.

However, many of the city's wild animals are more difficult to find. Some, like bats and many moths, are active only at night. They are *nocturnal,* and you would be very lucky to see them in daytime. Other plants and animals are so small that they may not be noticed. The green powder on the trunks of many trees is made up of hundreds of tiny plants called Pleurococcus. If you dig your garden, one spadeful of soil will contain thousands of tiny animals, including mites, springtails, worms and beetles.

What is a habitat?

The place where an animal or plant lives is called its *habitat.* This means its natural surroundings. It is easy to recognize many habitats in the countryside. Woodland, meadows, mountains and the seashore all provide different living conditions. Each is a habitat, and each has its own collection of animals and plants. Seaweed cannot live in a meadow and oak trees do not grow well on a seashore!

A city or town may look like a single habitat. However, urban animals and plants do not all live together. The house spider and cellar spider may be common in buildings, but they are not normally found in parks. The orb-web spider lives in shrubberies, but not usually in houses.

The city is not a single habitat, but a patchwork of different habitats. This patchwork may include parks, gardens, roads, walls and ponds. Each is a separate habitat, where a different group of animals and plants lives.

Any habitat, together with all the animals and plants to be found within it, is called an *ecosystem.* The garden pond with its fish, insects, snails and plants, is a very good example of an ecosystem. It is easy to study a pond because you can see where the water and land meet, showing the edge of the pond ecosystem.

▲ The sycamore is a common town tree. It has winged seeds, which whirl through the air in autumn.

Where do plants come from?

When builders finish work on a new house, they often simply level the ground which will be the garden and cover it with good soil. This makes a new habitat. Hundreds of different animals and plants could live in this new habitat. Several different species may try to occupy a particular spot. This race is called *competition.*

On bare ground, the race is usually won by small annual plants like shepherd's purse and knotgrass. This is because annuals produce enormous numbers of seeds, which are scattered over a wide area. Thousands of seeds may also be carried in with the new soil put down by the builders.

Animals move in

Where plants can grow, animals can live. The soil is full of tiny animals which eat plant remains. Snails, worms and slugs eat leaves and stems. They are eaten by larger animals, such as birds, who also use trees and shrubs as nesting places. In this way animals and plants colonize the new habitat at the same time.

In cities, living space for animals and plants may be more limited than it is in the countryside. However, every available living space is fully used by plants and animals.

Town and country

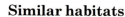

We all know the difference between towns and the countryside. Towns contain buildings, roads and railways. The countryside is open space, with few buildings. This may give us the wrong idea about the wildlife in each.

Natural or artificial?

Many people think that town habitats are all man-made, while habitats in the countryside are natural. This is not true. Almost all the countryside in Europe has been shaped by people. The natural land cover in most European countries is woodland. Over the past few hundred years, most of the trees have been cut down. Apart from mountain tops and the seashore, countryside habitats are as unnatural as those in towns.

Some city habitats may even be more 'natural' than the surrounding countryside. Every town has some areas of wasteland. This is land which has never been built on. Wasteland is often found beside railway sidings, inside factory fences or between blocks of buildings. Almost all the plants there have grown from seeds which were brought in by natural means, such as the wind, birds and animals. The land has not been treated with weedkillers or fertilizers. The result is a 'natural' community of plants and animals.

'Nothing lives in a town.'

Another common mistake is to believe that country habitats are rich in different species of plants and animals, while town habitats are not. In fact, many areas of the countryside are almost empty. For example, thousands of hectares of woodland have been planted with North American trees. Very few European animals can live there.

In contrast to these barren landscapes, many city habitats are very rich in species. A typical garden contains dozens of different plants, including shrubs and trees. These, in turn, provide food for hundreds of different invertebrates.

Similar habitats

Some areas of towns have many similarities to parts of the countryside. Roads, walls and roofs are like the bare rock of mountains and sea cliffs, and there is very little soil in which plants can take root. Many buildings have wide ledges, like the rock ledges on sea cliffs.

The animals and plants which live in the centre of cities are often ones that live on cliffs and mountains. Lichens and mosses grow on rooftops. Pigeons nest on the stone ledges on buildings. They are descended from rock doves, which live on rocky sea cliffs.

▼ **People in towns like to visit open green spaces. Parks imitate the countryside's water, grass and woodland, and provide a variety of different habitats.**

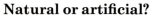

◀ Ledges on buildings are like those on sea-cliffs. Birds, such as starlings, use them as nesting and roosting sites. Thousands may roost on one building.

▶ Bats normally shelter in caves or hollow trees during the day and come out at night to hunt. In town centres many bats roost in towers and large buildings instead.

Some parts of the town, such as parks, are designed to be like countryside. Lawns represent pastureland, groves of trees imitate woodland, and shrubberies resemble the scrub which is often found at the edge of woodland. This variety of habitats attracts many animals.

Town habitats
Some habitats are only found in towns. Derelict land is land which has been used in the past, but is now lying idle, such as sites where buildings once stood.

Even if these derelict sites only lie idle for a few years before they are built on once again, they provide very important living spaces for city wildlife. Native plants like thistles, willowherb and grasses are very common. They hide the ugliness of derelict land and provide food for insects, which in turn are eaten by birds.

Another city habitat is the refuse tip. All the waste materials from houses, restaurants and food shops are food for birds and animals which scavenge on these tips, such as rats, gulls and crows. The rotting waste produces heat, so some insects which like warmth live here, such as cockroaches and house crickets.

Tips are also exciting places to look for plants. The refuse includes seeds of many kinds, such as seed from birdcages and spices from restaurants. These may germinate in the warmth so that plants from all over the world grow and flower on the rubbish.

Other habitats which are more common in towns than in the countryside include houses and other heated buildings and, of course, people. These all provide food and shelter for many different animals and plants.

How animals and plants arrive
Town habitats are colonized very quickly by animals and plants from the surrounding countryside. Many birds, insects and seeds fly in or are carried by the wind. Some come by water. They may drift down to the town from the upper reaches of a river. Others reach the dockland areas as accidental passengers in cargo ships.

Motorway verges, canal banks and railway embankments form green highways reaching from the heart of the country right into the city centre. These routes are followed by many of the larger animals. Foxes, in particular, travel by such routes.

This book looks at some town habitats and shows you many of the plants and animals living there. As you will see, studying wildlife in towns can be fascinating.

◀ Public and private gardens often contain rockeries. These copy the conditions on a mountain, where there is little soil and water drains away quickly.

▶ Artificial ponds and streams are very important nature reserves. Many natural pools in the countryside are disappearing as farmland is drained.

Exploring a park

Although they are artificial, parks can look very natural. They often contain several different countryside habitats, such as grassland, woodland and ponds.

▼ Honey bees

Honey bees are common visitors to flowers in parks. They start life as eggs, which are laid inside six-sided wax cells (1). The eggs hatch into larvae, which are fed on nectar and pollen collected from flowers (2). Some of the cells are used to store food for the winter (3).

▼ Froghopper

The nymphs suck sap from plant stems, and live inside a protective covering of foam, often called cuckoo spit. The adults (**right**) jump into the air when disturbed.

▼ Eyed hawkmoth

Willows are often planted beside lakes. Their leaves are eaten by eyed hawkmoth caterpillars. The adult shows pink hindwings with bright blue eyespots to frighten predators.

Key
1 Ash
2 Horse chestnut
3 Cedar of Lebanon
4 Crow
5 Fallow deer
6 Weeping willow
7 Herring gull
8 Magnolia
9 Maple
10 Oak
11 Black-headed gull
12 Teal
13 Coot
14 Male fern
15 Laurel
16 Viburnum
17 Berberis
18 Rabbit
19 Dabchick
20 Mute swan
21 Shelduck
22 Starling
23 Common shrew
24 Wren
25 Thrush
26 Fairy-ring toadstools
27 Hedge sparrow
28 Nuthatch
29 Squirrel
30 Hover-flies
31 Brimstone butterfly
32 Small copper butterfly
33 Common vole

The flowers in parks attract many **insects**, including butterflies (31, 32) and hover-flies (30). **Birds** come to feed on the insects. You may see nuthatches (28) and jays as well as starlings (22), thrushes (25) and crows (4).

Most parks have squirrels. Some also have deer.

▶ Mandarin duck

Ducks and other waterfowl are often introduced to lakes. One of the most attractive introduced species is the mandarin duck, originally from China and Japan. It is now widely bred in Europe, and normally nests in trees.

Trees

Trees are an important part of the city landscape. They give food and shelter to a variety of insects, and birds nest in them. Many have beautiful flowers or fruit, which add colour to the street.

*Not to scale. The maximum height is given.

▲ **Sycamore** 30m
A large, spreading tree, often planted in parks. It also grows easily and quickly wherever the winged fruits land. In early summer it has small flowers.

▼ **Silver birch** 30m
A graceful tree with silvery bark. Catkins appear in early summer and are followed by winged seeds. Many moth caterpillars eat the leaves.

▲ **Common or pedunculate oak** 45m
A large, deciduous tree with spreading branches and a huge trunk. It has acorns on long stalks in autumn, and is often found in parks.

▲ **Rowan, Mountain ash** 20m
This beautiful tree is said to bring good luck if planted in a garden. It has orange berries which blackbirds and thrushes eat in winter, and will grow well in poor soil.

▼ **Robinia, Locust, False acacia** 30m
Sweet-scented white flowers produce long seed-pods, which often stay throughout winter.

▼ **Catalpa, Indian bean tree** 15m
From North America. Large sprays of spotted flowers appear in late summer and produce thin seed pods, which can be 35cm long.

▲ **Beech** 40m
Beech leaves grow so thickly that they cut out light, preventing other plants growing underneath the tree. It has hard triangular nuts in prickly cases, which split when ripe.

▲ **Ash** 40m
A tall tree with smooth grey bark and black winter buds. There are several attractive varieties, including the weeping ash. The fruits each have a wing, and are called *keys*.

▲ Maidenhair tree, Gingko 30m

A very old Chinese tree, whose fossil remains have been found in rocks which are millions of years old. Its fan-shaped leaves have no central rib.

▲ Whitebeam 20m

This is often planted as a decorative tree. Its leaves have white undersides, which show when the wind blows. In autumn it has orange-red berries.

▲ Hornbeam 30m

A small tree or shrub with smooth grey bark, often planted in small open spaces. Its tiny green flowers produce hard nuts, each surrounded by a three-lobed wing.

▼ Scots pine 35m

This tree is often planted in parks and gardens. It has scaly, reddish bark and short blue-green needles, which grow in pairs.

▼ Corsican pine 35m

Another common ornamental evergreen tree. Its needles are up to 15cm long and grow in pairs. This tree originally came from Southern Europe.

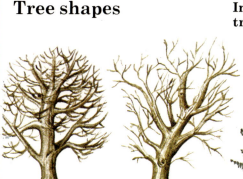

▲ Cedar of Lebanon 40m

A large, spreading tree, often found in parks. Short dark-green needles grow in upright clusters, and it has tight, barrel-shaped cones.

▲ Metasequoia, Dawn redwood 19m

Thought to be extinct, this evergreen was re-discovered in China in 1945. It can now be found growing in many city parks.

Tree shapes

In winter you can identify trees by their shapes.

Horse chestnut   Oak   Norway spruce   Ash

Every tree grows in a different way. Branches may be straight or twisted, drooping or upright. The outline of the tree may be wide and spreading or thin and compact.

These are some common trees in winter.

Spring

▲ These plants flower before trees grow leaves, so that they receive as much light as possible.
1 Bluebell   2 Primrose
3 Crocus   4 Snowdrop

Even in the centre of large cities, the signs of spring are unmistakable. The sun rises earlier and sets later, climbing a little higher in the sky each day. Slowly, the soil warms up and new growth appears.

The first plants
Amongst the early signs of spring are the bursting silver-grey buds of the pussy willow or great sallow. This can be found growing in parks and beside streams on city commons. The silver buds burst open to expose the bright yellow catkins. Pollen from these catkins is carried by the wind to the much smaller female catkins on a nearby tree.

As the spring sunshine warms the soil, the trees of the city streets begin to grow again. The roots take water from the soil. This water carries food from the roots up to the branches and the leaves begin to unfold.

The warmth of the soil also stimulates seeds into growth. All over the soil of wasteland, parks and gardens, there are millions of seeds left from the previous year. The warm spring sun and moisture from the spring rains are all that is needed to make these seeds germinate and start growing. Bare soil is quickly covered with a green carpet.

Animals in spring
As the plants begin to grow again and the first flowers open, insects become more active. Many butterflies and moths which have passed the winter as pupae emerge, mate and lay eggs. The large white butterfly may be on the wing in March. The small tortoiseshell and peacock butterflies also hibernate, as do ladybirds.

As the season continues, many hawkmoths emerge from their underground pupae and visit the garden borders at night.

The longer hours of daylight signal the start of the breeding season for the city's birds. This is the time when bird song is at its best. The song thrush and blackbird will choose treetops or other high spots from which they will sing loudly from early morning and often late in the evening. Sometimes, a bird will be confused by street lights and a blackbird may be heard singing in the middle of the night.

▲ These trees have flowers before leaves, so that the pollen is easily blown from the male flowers on to the females.
1 Pussy willow   2 Hazel

▲ Swallows build open mud nests under the roofs of houses, often in small groups. The female usually lays between four and seven eggs, which both parents incubate.

Bird song is very important. It is one way in which a bird claims a piece of land as its own territory. A male bird that has claimed a territory will attract a female. They will select a nest site and begin to build a nest. The eggs are soon laid and incubation begins.

Many mammals remain active all through the winter, but those which have hibernated emerge in spring. They hurry to find food to put on the weight that they have lost during hibernation. Grey squirrels, hedgehogs and bats all spend the winter asleep.

Foreign visitors
In late spring and early summer, summer migrants arrive. These are birds and insects which cannot usually survive through the winter in western Europe, and come here just for the breeding season. Best known of the migrants are the swallow, swift and house martin.

Swifts scream almost non-stop as they fly in small flocks all over the town. They make their nests on the walls of buildings. Swallows often build their nests inside large buildings, while house martins build their mud nests under the eaves of houses.

Summer

Spring blends gently into summer, when the days are long and warm. Gardens and parks are bright with flowers. Many flowering plants depend on insects to carry pollen from one flower to another. This process, called *pollination,* is necessary before seeds can develop.

Flowers which are pollinated by day-flying insects are usually brightly coloured. Those which depend on night-flying insects are often strongly scented, although this scent will attract bees and flies in daytime as well.

Insects visit the flowers in search of food. This is produced in the form of nectar, a sugary liquid. As they try to reach the nectar, insects brush against the anthers of the flower. Grains of pollen from the anthers are caught in the hairs on the insects' bodies, and are carried to another flower as the insects look for more nectar. Some insects, including the honey bee, collect pollen from garden flowers and carry it back to their nests as food for their larvae.

▲ These are cultivated flowers, which are planted in parks and gardens.
1 Snapdragon 2 Aster 3 Zinnia
4 French marigold 5 Begonia
6 Rose

Insects everywhere

Many of the more common insects, such as aphids, are too successful in the summer. They can breed very quickly and can become pests to a gardener. However, aphids are very important to the natural history of towns. They provide food for many other insects, including ladybirds, lacewings and hover-flies, so without them a garden cannot support as many different animals.

▲ A red admiral sunning itself on an evening primrose. Butterflies are attracted to flowers by their scent more than by their colour, which they see differently from us.

Other insect pests attack both flowers and vegetables. Among the best known are the caterpillars (larvae) of the large and small white butterflies. The caterpillars of the small white are green and feed singly. Those of the large white are greenish-grey, with yellow lines and black dots, and they feed in groups. Both species can do serious damage to cabbages. In turn, they are eaten by the larvae of parasitic wasps.

Some gardeners try to control pests by spraying plants with insecticides. This must be done carefully. Careless spraying can kill useful insects – bees, ladybirds, hover-flies, parasitic wasps – as well as the pests.

▲ A sparrow feeding its half-grown chicks. They can fly short distances with their small, stumpy wings. However, they still demand food all day long.

Birds in summer

At the height of summer, almost no birdsong can be heard in towns. Many birds have left gardens to build nests where they can be undisturbed. Those that remain become quiet and secretive. When there are young birds in the nest, both parents must visit them with food every few minutes from dawn to dusk. They hunt quietly in order to avoid attracting attention to their young.

As the season progresses, young birds can often be found learning to fly, unaccompanied by their parents. After leaving the nest, the young will still be fed by their parents until they have learned to find food.

Every year, thousands of young birds are 'rescued' by people. Most of these rescued birds die, because people cannot give them enough of the right food at the right times. Unless they are injured, these birds should be left alone. Their parents will feed them until they can look after themselves.

So summer is a time of great activity, with plants growing fast, insects multiplying and both mammals and birds busy looking after their young.

Waste-land

Waste and derelict land are very valuable nature reserves in most towns and cities. Plants and animals can live there almost unaffected by people. The grass is not mown and shrubs are not pruned. Plants are not destroyed by weedkillers and insecticides are not used. Animals can breed and raise their young without being disturbed.

▲ Caterpillars

Nettles are eaten by many caterpillars. This is the caterpillar of the peacock butterfly, which is often found in groups. Red admiral and small tortoiseshell butterflies also lay their eggs on nettles.

Key

1 Redstart	13 Dead nettle
2 Nettles	14 Lupin
3 Sowthistle	15 Wren
4 Herring gull	16 Starlings
5 Oxford ragwort	17 Opium poppy
6 Crows	18 Ragwort
7 Rowan	19 False oat grass
8 Silver birch	20 Soft brome
9 Kestrel	21 Brambles
10 Hawthorn	22 Yorkshire fog
11 Badger sett	23 Scentless mayweed
12 Buddleia	24 Rosebay willowherb

▼ A **black redstart** (1) sings from a broken gutter. This handsome bird nests in holes in walls and usually eats insects

▼ Mosquitoes and midges

The common gnat (1) breeds in any still water. The eggs hatch into larvae (2), which feed head-down in the water, taking in air through a tube. The pupa (3) hangs just below the surface. The adult female feeds on the blood of birds. On the right is a midge.

► A **kestrel** (9) hovers over the railway embankment, looking for mice or voles. It nests on the ledges of large buildings.

▼ **Butterflies**
Buddleia (12) attracts many insects, particularly butterflies. The red admiral may have migrated from southern Europe. Small tortoiseshells spend the winter here.

Red admiral butterfly

Small tortoiseshell butterfly

▼ **Elephant hawkmoth caterpillar on rosebay willowherb (24)**
The 'eyes' of the caterpillar are not real, but just protective colouring. The adult moths fly at night, hovering while they drink nectar from flowers.

A rich variety of **plants** grows on undisturbed wasteland, and provides food for many different animals. The first plants to arrive often include shepherd's purse, groundsel, fat-hen, annual meadow grass, knotgrass and chickweed. They cover the soil quickly, then slower-growing plants can take root. Scentless mayweed (23) and ragwort (18) mingle with pink rosebay willowherb (24) and even, occasionally, a purple opium

poppy (17). More permanent grasses arrive, such as soft brome (20), false oat grass (19) and Yorkshire fog (22).

Insects and birds feed on the plants. Small trees, like rowan (7), silver birch (8) and hawthorn (10), grow on embankments. Under them mice, voles and rabbits find shelter, and badgers may dig their setts (11).

17

Flowers of the wasteland

An interesting mixture of plants grows on wasteland. Some are common in the countryside, others have escaped from gardens. *Not to scale. Average height given.

◀ Chickweed 5–40cm
This tiny trailing plant is a very common annual. It grows quickly on bare soil in parks, gardens and on wasteland.

▶ Honesty 30–100cm
Originally a garden plant. In early summer it has purple or white flowers. The silvery flat seed pods are often used for decoration.

▶ Knotgrass 30cm when upright
This annual is often one of the first plants to colonize waste ground or bare soil in gardens. It usually trails along the ground.

◀ Sorrel 10–100cm
The green flower spikes appear in early summer, then change to red. The leaves have a lemony taste and can be added to salads.

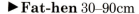

◀ Rosebay willowherb, Fireweed 30–120cm
Often found in large clumps, with tall spires of pink flowers or fluffy seeds. One of the first plants to grow after a fire.

▶ Large bindweed 1–3m
The trumpet-shaped flowers each last for only one day. It spreads by long, creeping underground stems, which are very difficult to dig out.

▶ Fat-hen 30–90cm
A common weed of gardens, fat-hen will also colonize disturbed ground on derelict sites. Its green flower spikes grow in summer. The mealy green leaves used to be eaten as a vegetable.

◀ Shepherd's purse 3–40cm
A common plant which has tiny white flowers throughout the year. Its heart-shaped seedpods look like the purses once carried by shepherds. They split when ripe.

◀ Ivy-leaved toadflax 60cm
A dainty little trailing plant with lilac and yellow flowers in summer. Its leaves look like those of ivy. It was originally grown in gardens, but is now found on many walls.

▶ **Ribwort plantain** 40cm
A perennial weed of lawns and roadside verges. The leaves grow in a flat rosette. In summer tall stalks grow from the centre with spikes of tiny brownish flowers.

▶ **Creeping buttercup** 15cm
This pretty plant flowers throughout the summer. It is a troublesome weed in gardens, because it spreads so well. It sends out runners from which new plants grow.

◀ **Goldenrod** 60–250cm
This is a garden plant which often escapes to wasteland. It has tiny yellow flowers which grow in clusters, and long thin leaves. It spreads by underground stems.

◀ **Common ragwort** 30-150cm
This common plant has many bright yellow flower-heads on branched stems. It is eaten by the black and orange striped caterpillars of the cinnabar moth.

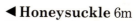

▶ **Spear thistle** 50–150cm
This tall prickly plant with sharp toothed leaves is common on wasteland and by roads. The flower-heads produce fluffy seeds which blow away in autumn or are eaten by goldfinches.

▶ **Michaelmas daisy** 40–120cm
An old-fashioned garden plant which grows in clumps. In autumn it has clusters of sweet-scented flowers, which attract small tortoiseshell butterflies.

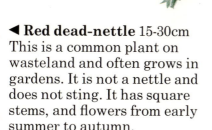

◀ **Red dead-nettle** 15-30cm
This is a common plant on wasteland and often grows in gardens. It is not a nettle and does not sting. It has square stems, and flowers from early summer to autumn.

◀ **Honeysuckle** 6m
This sweetly-scented climber often grows on undisturbed derelict land. Moths feed on the flowers at night. In autumn it has red berries.

Grasses
The commonest wild flowers in towns are rarely noticed. These are the grasses, which grow everywhere.
    The five above are often found.
1 Couch 150cm **2** Wild barley 50cm
3 Perennial rye 50cm **4** Cock's-foot 100cm
5 Yorkshire fog 100cm

▶ **Bird's foot trefoil** 10-40cm
This attractive little trailing plant grows on wasteland and as a weed in lawns. The flowers are yellow, with red tips, and grow in clusters. In autumn they become long seedpods which look like birds' feet. It has many different names, for example *Bacon and eggs* and *Lady's slipper*.

Day and night

Although there are a few animals which are active by both day and night, most are either *diurnal* (active by day) or *nocturnal* (active by night). The garden is full of life and activity all the time, but most of the animals seen by day are different from those seen at night.

Adult   Aphids

Larva

▲ Ladybird and larvae
These colourful little beetles are fierce hunters. Both adults and larvae feed on aphids. The larvae are blue-grey. Ladybirds are usually red or yellow with black spots but can be black with red or yellow spots.

Peacock butterfly

Hummingbird hawkmoth

Bumble bee

Orange tip butterfly

Hover-fly

◀ Dozens of different **insects** visit one flower-head in a day. You may see hover-flies (22), bumble bees (21), peacock (10) and orange tip (11) butterflies.

Birds are everywhere in the daytime. A song thrush (19) cracks snail shells and a blackbird (14) hunts for worms. A house martin (7) swoops after insects, a blue tit (2) picks up insects from the laburnum tree (1) and a collared dove (4) looks for seeds.

▲ Wolf spider
This active spider hunts insects by day and night. You may see it on open spaces, such as flower beds, rocks and fences, particularly in sunshine. It does not spin a web, but leaps on its prey. The female carries the egg cocoon. When the young hatch they ride on her back.

▶ Many **moths** visit gardens at night. They can 'smell' scent from the flowers with their antennae. Some common moths are the puss moth (26), red underwing (7), garden tiger (16) and elephant hawkmoth (24).

Few birds are seen at night, but **mammals** are very active. Bats (6) chase flying insects, and owls (5) hunt small animals. Rats (25) scavenge in the compost heap and a hedgehog (15) hunts worms and slugs on the lawn.

Puss moth

Red underwing moth

Elephant hawkmoth

Garden tiger moth

Small mammals

Although many different mammals live in towns, they are not often seen. This is because most of them are *nocturnal* (active at night). Squirrels are an exception, and can be seen throughout the day. Others, like rabbits and hedgehogs, may be seen in the evening or early morning.

*Not to scale. The size given is the body-length of an adult including tail.

How a bat finds food

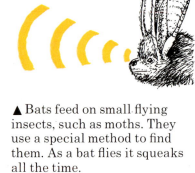

▲ Bats feed on small flying insects, such as moths. They use a special method to find them. As a bat flies it squeaks all the time.

▲ If these sounds hit an insect, some of them are reflected back to the bat. It follows the echoes to the insect.

▼ **Shrew** 90–120mm
This tiny mammal feeds on slugs, worms and insects. It has a very large appetite and often hunts during the day. The shrew has poor eyesight, but a keen sense of smell. It can be distinguished from mice and voles by its very pointed nose and dark brown fur.

▼ **Long-tailed field mouse** 150–225mm
A common garden animal, the field mouse often makes its home in a garden shed, and will sometimes come into a house in winter. It feeds on plants and seeds.

▼ **House mouse** 140–180mm
This mouse lives in walls and under floors. It feeds on food scraps and stored food, and may spread diseases. Some house mice have adapted to life in refrigerated food stores.

▲ **Field vole** 120–150mm
Occasionally seen in daylight. It feeds on plants and seeds, and can be a nuisance because it eats vegetables and flower bulbs. The vole's small ears, rounded nose and short tail distinguish it from mice.

▼ **Brown rat** 360–500mm
This pest has adapted very well to life in towns. It lives in drains and sewers, factories and wasteland, eats anything and scavenges in dustbins and waste tips. It damages stored food and carries diseases.

▲ **Black rat** 350–480mm
This unwelcome pest has been spread all over the world by ships. It lives in buildings, such as dockland warehouses. It can cause serious damage to stored food and spreads disease.

▲ Red squirrel 370–500mm
This rodent eats seeds, fruit, tree-buds and birds' eggs. In winter it sleeps in a hole in a tree, and wakes on sunny days.

▲ Grey squirrel 460–500mm
Originally from North America. It is a popular animal in parks, taking food from visitors. Like the red squirrel, it is mainly vegetarian and hoards food. It sleeps in winter, but is active on mild days.

▼ Long-eared bat 80–100mm
Can be distinguished by its broad wings and long ears. This bat is normally nocturnal and spends the day hidden in a hollow tree, or in a loft or church steeple. It feeds on flying insects.

▼ Pipistrelle bat 60–80mm
A furry bat, more often seen than the long-eared bat because it flies at dusk. It roosts in groups in buildings during the day. In winter it hibernates.

▲ Rabbit 400mm
This furry pet can be a pest in the countryside. In towns it lives on commons, in parks, in suburban areas with large gardens or on railway embankments. It feeds on a variety of plants, which can make it unpopular with gardeners.

▲ Hedgehog 160–260mm
Hunts insects, worms and slugs in the evening or early morning, finding its food by smell. Its spines protect it from enemies. It hibernates in dry sheltered places, such as in piles of leaves or under sheds.

▼ Fox 100cm
This large animal eats small mammals, particularly field voles, but also scavenges from dustbins and waste tips. The fox often makes its home, called an earth, by enlarging a rabbit hole.

▼ Badger 750–930mm
This large mammal is rarely seen. It sometimes makes its home, or sett, on a quiet railway embankment. It is nocturnal, and eats almost anything.

The road-side

Up to a quarter of the ground space in towns is taken up by roads and car parks. Even though most of the soil in these is covered by tarmac or concrete, many different plants and animals survive in these harsh conditions.

▲ Aphids on a lime leaf
Millions of aphids may live on a single large lime tree, feeding on its sap. As they feed, they produce a sugary liquid called honeydew. Ants feed on this, as do several fungi. The aphids are also eaten by insects and birds.

Roof tiles and walls are like the bare rock of mountains and sea cliffs. Very few plants live there. However, one group of plants that can grow in these dry conditions are the **lichens** (11) such as blackshields and yellowscales. Lichens are killed by pollution.

Walls also provide a niche for **plants** which need little soil. You may find fleshy-leaved stonecrop (10), with white or yellow flowers, and dainty ivy-leaved toadflax (14).

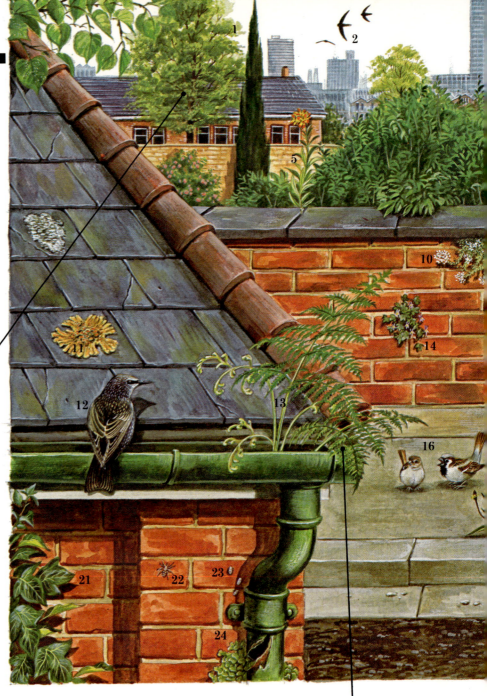

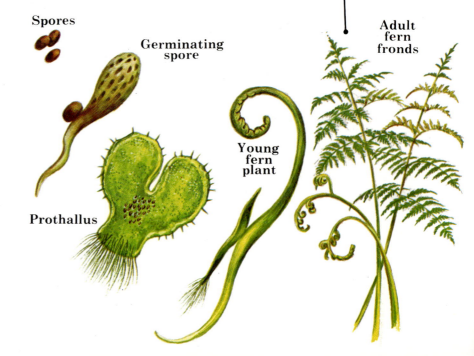

Spores

Germinating spore

Prothallus

Young fern plant

Adult fern fronds

▼ Privet hawkmoth caterpillar

One common hedge plant is privet, which provides food for these large green caterpillars. At the end of the summer, the caterpillar burrows into the soil and turns into a pupa. In spring the moth will emerge.

Small tough **plants** grow in cracks in the pavement and gutter. Plantains (20), dandelions (17), clover (18), daisies (19), shepherd's purse (15) and some grasses (26) all manage to flower in these tiny pockets of soil.

◀ Ferns

Some tough plants, such as bracken (13), can grow in gutters. Bracken is a fern. Tiny spores are blown into the gutter, where each grows into a small green heart-shaped plant called a prothallus. After a few weeks, a small fern plant begins to grow on the prothallus, which then disappears.

▶ Mosses

Mosses (8) grow in crevices in walls. Two of the commonest ones are wall screw moss (above) and silvery thread moss (below). The moss traps brick particles, which start to form soil.

Key	
1	Lime
2	Swift
3	Pigeon
4	Cherry
5	Wallflower
6	Privet
7	Lime
8	Moss
9	Wolf spider
10	Stonecrop
11	Lichens
12	Starling
13	Bracken
14	Ivy-leaved toadflax
15	Shepherd's purse
16	Sparrow
17	Dandelion
18	Clover
19	Daisy
20	Plantain
21	Ivy
22	Zebra spider
23	Woodlice
24	Liverwort
25	Pied wagtail
26	Grass

Insects and other tiny animals

Invertebrates live everywhere. Some are large, others too small to see without a microscope. Some fly, others live on or under the ground.

*Not to scale. Adult body-length given.

▲ Hawthorn shieldbug 17mm
This common shieldbug has piercing and sucking mouthparts, and looks like a shield. It feeds on hawthorn berries. In spring it also eats leaves.

▲ Ichneumon fly 17mm
Most ichneumon flies are parasites on other insects. The females lay their eggs in the body of a moth or butterfly larva. When the eggs hatch they feed on the body of the caterpillar. This ichneumon fly often flies into houses at dusk.

▲ Common field grasshopper 17mm
Often seen or heard in summer in rough grass on wasteland. It eats plants, mainly grass, and is usually brown, sometimes with green patches.

▼ Lime hawkmoth 35mm
Adult moths fly at night in early summer. They vary in colour and pattern. The larvae are bright green with yellow markings, and feed on lime leaves.

▼ Drone-fly 25mm
This is a hover-fly, and can be seen flying or hovering in the garden on a warm summer day. It looks like a bee, but has no sting, and only one pair of wings.

▼ Oak-apple gall wasp 3mm
The female wasp lays eggs in the buds of the oak, which makes galls form. The larvae mature inside the galls and adult wasps emerge in summer.

▼ Wall brown butterfly wingspan 47mm
On sunny days this butterfly can be seen flying on open grassy wasteland. Its larvae feed on grasses at night.

▲ **Centipede** 5–10mm
This is not an insect, because it has more than six legs. It spends the day hiding. At night it hunts spiders, insects and small slugs. It has one pair of legs on each body segment.

▼ **Orb-web spider** 5–12mm
This beautiful garden spider spins a large sticky web, and hides in nearby leaves. Insects are trapped in the web and the spider feeds on them.

▲ **Common wasp** 11–20mm
Wasps live in nests underground, or in walls. They live mainly on nectar and rotting fruit. They only sting in self-defence. The larvae are fed on flies.

▲ **Millipede** 17–20m
This invertebrate is slower-moving than a centipede and usually eats rotting plants. It has two pairs of legs on each segment.

▼ **Harvestman** 4-9mm
The harvestman can be seen quite often in daylight. It runs over the ground or scrambles through plants hunting for the flies and ants which it eats.

▲ **Red-tailed bumble bee** 22mm
This large bee usually nests in an old mouse-hole underground, in colonies of several hundred bees. The larvae are fed on honey.

▲ **Earwig** 12mm
Feeds mainly on insects, which it hunts at night. Its name probably comes from its ear-shaped wings. The female earwig guards her eggs and young until they are fully grown.

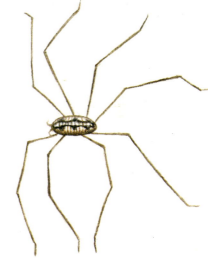

▼ **Cockchafer, Maybug (male)** 24mm
This large beetle flies at night and often crashes into lighted windows. The larvae live in the soil, feeding on grass roots. The male has 'fans' on his antennae.

Camouflage

Some animals avoid being eaten by being hard to see against their background.

The peppered moth often rests on silver birch trees during the day, and is white with black spots (**left**). In cities a new form has developed, which is black (**right**). This is so that the moth cannot be seen against the dirty tree-trunks.

Along the canal

Before the railways were built, canals were the most important means of transporting heavy goods. Today, most goods are carried by road or rail. However, many canals are still used, either for transport or by pleasure boats.

Others have become stretches of stagnant water. Where they run through industrial cities canals may be polluted. The cleaner a canal is, the more life it contains.

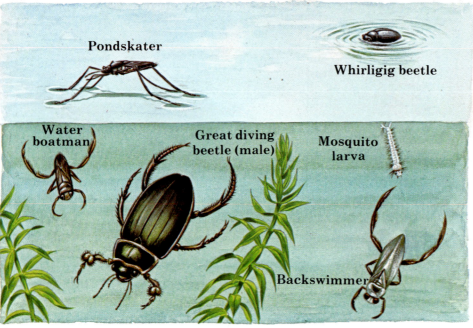

Pondskater

Whirligig beetle

Water boatman

Great diving beetle (male)

Mosquito larva

Backswimmer

▲ On the surface
Some animals live only on the surface of the water. Others swim freely, while some crawl on plants or the canal bottom.

One very common surface-animal is the pondskater (18). This insect skims about on the surface film, and can move very quickly to capture insects or other small animals at the surface of the water. The pondskater is often joined by groups of whirligig beetles (19) which swim in circles on the surface of the water.

◄ Underwater
Below the surface the canal teems with life. Many insects which swim freely have to return to the surface to obtain fresh supplies of air. The fiercest of these is the great diving beetle (24), which will attack fish much larger than itself.

Another active hunter is the backswimmer (22). Swimming upside-down, propelled by two long oar-like legs, the backswimmer hunts for tadpoles, beetle larvae and small fish. The water boatman (20) is smaller and flatter.

The canal and banks provide food and shelter for many **birds,** such as reed buntings (5) and moorhens (14).

Insects swarm above the water and are caught by swallows (3). Yellow wagtails (8) arrive in summer and feed on insects. Herons (7) fish in the shallows.

▼ **Flatworms, snails, leeches**
Flatworms (**1**) feed on water fleas and other small animals.

Snails eat small plants which grow on larger plants.

Leeches (**2**) attack fish, tadpoles and even snails, and suck out blood and body fluids.

Ramshorn snail

Wandering snail

Key

1 Alder	**13** Arrowhead
2 Willow	**14** Moorhen
3 Swallow	**15** Starwort
4 Guelder rose	**16** Yellow water-lily
5 Reed bunting	**17** Ramshorn snail
6 Common reed	**18** Pond skater
7 Heron	**19** Whirligig beetle
8 Yellow wagtail	**20** Water boatman
9 Rosebay	**21** Mosquito larva
willowherb	**22** Backswimmer
10 Comfrey	**23** Carp
11 Rush	**24** Great diving beetle
12 Great marsh sedge	**25** Eel
	26 Canadian pondweed
	27 Yellow flag

◄ On the bottom

The water scorpion (**1**) hides in plants just below the surface, with a long breathing tube pushed up through the surface film. It seizes small animals such as fish and tadpoles. Dragonfly nymphs (**2**) also hunt among the plants and on the canal bed. They have extending lower jaws, called a mask, which they shoot out to seize passing animals.

Another crawling animal is the water louse (**3**). This relative of the woodlouse feeds on decaying animals and plants.

The banks are often covered with a thick mass of **plants** such as thistles, nettles, rosebay and great willowherb and meadowsweet. Trees that prefer damp soil, including willows (2) and alder (1), grow well on canal banks, as do many of the smaller hedgerow trees, such as wayfaring tree and guelder rose.

Water voles live among the plants, nesting in holes in the bank. These mammals swim very well. Their coats look silvery under water, as the fur traps bubbles of air.

Life in the water

Hundreds of different animals and plants live in a canal.

*Not to scale.

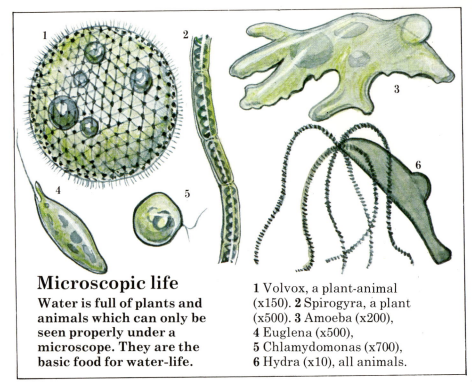

Microscopic life
Water is full of plants and animals which can only be seen properly under a microscope. They are the basic food for water-life.

1 Volvox, a plant-animal (x150). 2 Spirogyra, a plant (x500). 3 Amoeba (x200), 4 Euglena (x500), 5 Chlamydomonas (x700), 6 Hydra (x10), all animals.

▲ **Water milfoil** life-size
A common water plant, which grows rooted in mud at the bottom of ponds, canals and streams. Its feathery leaves make a great deal of oxygen during daylight.

▲ **Water starwort** life-size
Another common underwater plant which grows on mud. At the end of each stem are four leaves which grow in a star-shape.

▲ **Canadian pondweed** life-size
You will find this plant in most freshwater habitats. It grows completely underwater except for its tiny pinkish flowers, which float on the surface.

▶ **Great diving beetle** 25mm
One of the most savage underwater predators is the great diving beetle. Both the nymphs and adults are carnivorous and will attack larger animals.

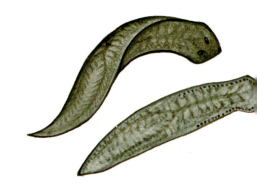

▲ **Flatworms: dugesia (top), polycelis (bottom)** 15mm
These are normally found under stones or on the underside of leaves. They feed on small animals and their eggs.

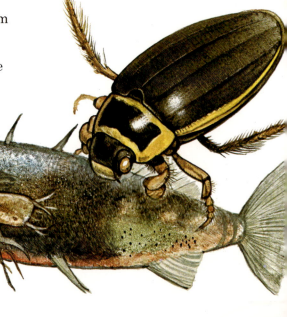

▲ **Damselfly laying eggs** 45mm
Damselfly eggs hatch into wingless nymphs, which live underwater until ready to become adults.

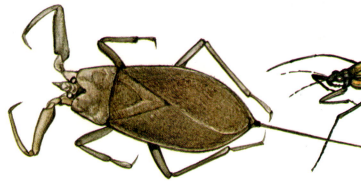

▲**Water scorpion (left)** 25mm, **pondskater (right)** 20mm
The water scorpion and pondskater are both bugs. Their front wings are toughened and protect the thinner hind wings.

The slow-moving water scorpion lives below the surface, and breathes through its long tube. The quicker pondskater skims over the surface film on its long legs. Both eat other insects.

▲ **Water boatman (left)** 20mm, **backswimmer (right)** 20mm
The water boatman looks silver underwater, and the backswimmer swims on its back. Both are fierce hunters. They pierce small animals with their sharp mouthparts and suck out their juices.

▲ **Newts** life-size
The palmate newt (top) is the smallest of these three newts. The male has webbed hind feet. The common newt (bottom) is slightly larger. In the breeding season the male grows a crest from nose to tail. The largest of all is the great crested newt (right), which has a high, ragged crest.

Newts live on land but return to the water to breed. The great crested newt spends more time in the water than do the other two.

▲**Water spider** 8-15mm
This is the only spider in the world which can live underwater. The water spider spins a web on water plants and fills it with air from the surface.

▼ **Common frog (left)** 10cm, **common toad (right)** 12cm
The common frog has a smooth moist skin and normally lives in very damp places near water.

The toad has a rough, warty skin and is often found in dry places. The frog usually hops and the toad usually walks. Both feed on insects and breed in water.

Autumn

As summer ends the days grow shorter. The sun is slightly lower in the sky each day and, although the days may still be warm, the nights are becoming colder. Autumn has arrived and, as it does, the pace of life begins to slow down.

The main flowering season is now over. Many flowers have been successfully pollinated, either by the summer breezes or by the hordes of insects which have visited them.

Once they have been pollinated the flowers die and their seeds begin to ripen. Some plants drop their ripe seeds on to the soil below. They will lie there until the warmth and rains of the spring help them to germinate and grow into new plants.

Seed dispersal
Because they are near the parent plant, and near each other, the tiny plants will have to fight for light, air and food. Many plants have developed ways of

▲ **Before swallows migrate they gather in large flocks, often on telegraph wires.**

spreading their seeds over a wider area, so that each plant gets more space.

Many plants use the wind to spread their seeds. Dandelions, rosebay willowherb, ragwort, groundsel and thistles all have fluffy seeds which are blown away by the wind. This is a very effective way of spreading seeds, and is why these plants are so good at colonizing wasteland.

Birds and other animals also play an important part in seed dispersal. Seeds of plants like blackberry, apple, mountain ash, hawthorn and mistletoe are surrounded by juicy fruits, which are often eaten by birds. As the fruit passes through the bird's body only the soft parts are digested. The seed is passed out of the body undamaged, far away from where it was eaten.

Goosegrass, or cleavers, is a common plant of waste places. Its seeds are enclosed in small green fruits, which are covered with small hooked hairs. When an animal brushes against the plant, these hooked hairs catch in its fur and can be carried a long way before the seeds fall to the ground.

Leaf fall
As fruits and seeds ripen and fall, many plants begin to lose their leaves. Trees which do this are called *deciduous*. Waste materials from the trunk and branches are passed into the leaves, and the chemicals in the leaves themselves begin to break down. These often produce beautiful colours.

After a few days they all leave at once on their long flight south to warmer countries.

As this happens the bottom of each leaf stalk becomes soft, and is sealed off from the tree by a layer of cork. Before the dead leaf is finally blown off the tree the cork forms a protective layer which keeps disease out. By the end of autumn these trees are in a resting (*dormant*) state which will continue until the spring.

Fungi
Autumn is the best season of the year for fungi, such as mushrooms and toadstools. These plants cannot make their own food, but feed mainly on other plants and animals. Many fungi feed on rotting plants, which are everywhere in autumn.

▲ **Some fruits are hard, some have wings and some grow in bunches. Some are scattered by the wind, others by birds.
1 Horse chestnut 2 Rowan 3 Sycamore 4 Elder 5 Ash**

▲ **Some common fungi.
1 Fly agaric, a poisonous toadstool. 2 Shaggy ink cap, found on wasteland. 3 Coral spot, a tiny fungus which grows on dead wood.**

Winter

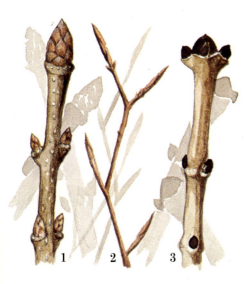

▲ You can identify trees in winter by the shape and arrangement of their buds. Look for these three. 1 Horse chestnut 2 Beech 3 Ash

What happens to plants?

Winter is a resting time for plants. Annuals die, leaving seeds to grow into new plants in spring. Many other plants die down above ground but have underground roots or food stores from which new shoots appear.

In many city gardens and on rubbish dumps there are plants from warmer parts of the world which can survive the cold winter. This is because a town is always warmer than the surrounding countryside. The buildings provide many south-facing walls, where plants can be sheltered from the worst of the cold northerly winds, while the heat escaping from thousands of buildings warms the air.

Animals in winter

Throughout autumn, hedgehogs are often active in the garden early in the evening. They are feeding heavily to build up layers of fat which will carry them through the winter months.

Towards the end of autumn, they hide away in ditches and under garden sheds. Their hearts and breathing slow down and their body temperature drops. They remain in this state until spring.

Grey squirrels spend the winter in hollow trees, and bats gather in large colonies under the roofs of old buildings.

How birds survive

As the weather grows colder, summer migrants prepare to leave. The lower temperature quickly reduces the population of insects and as their food disappears, swallows, house martins and swifts gather for their long flight south.

Although summer migrants have left, town gardens are still full of birds. Town birds have a better chance of survival than their country cousins because towns are warmer and people feed birds. Many birds that have spent the summer and autumn in the country move into towns for the winter.

You will see many more birds in winter if your garden has a bird table. Blue tits, great tits and coal tits hunt through shrubs and tree trunks for over-wintering insects and visit bird tables for peanuts and bacon rinds. Starlings and house sparrows squabble over almost any food. Blackbirds and greenfinches will visit bird tables regularly, while chaffinches, song thrushes, pied wagtails and meadow pipits prefer to hunt on the ground for scraps.

▲ The redwing (top) and fieldfare (bottom) spend most of the year in Scandinavia. They are too shy to visit gardens, but you may see them in parks.

Birds which live here throughout the year are called *residents.* In winter they are joined by migrants from colder countries further north. Regular visitors to cities include fieldfares and redwings, relatives of blackbirds and thrushes. Sometimes you may also see the beautiful waxwing.

City lakes and reservoirs provide a winter home for many different water birds. Mallard and tufted duck are joined by winter visitors, including pintail, shoveler, wigeon and teal.

Even in winter, our towns are full of wildlife.

▲ Many animals spend the winter in a deep sleep, though some wake up on warm days.

1 Grey squirrel in its drey. 2 Hedgehog curled up in dead leaves. 3 Frog buried in mud.

Birds

Town birds come from many different habitats but all have learned to live with people.

*Not to scale. Adult body-length given.

▲House martin 12–13cm
Originally a cliff and cave-nesting species. House martins live in mud nests which they build under the eaves of houses. They migrate south in autumn.

▲Feral pigeon 31–34cm
These large birds are descended from rock doves. They vary in colour and pattern, and can be seen everywhere in towns. They nest on buildings.

▲House sparrow 14–15cm
This is a true town bird. It spends most of its life near to houses, and lives almost entirely on scraps from houses. It makes an untidy nest in a hole, often in a building.

▲Blue tit 11–12cm
This woodland bird is often seen in town gardens. It is mainly an insect eater, but also takes peanuts and bacon rind from bird tables in winter.

▲Blackbird 24–26cm
The cock bird is black with a yellow bill, and the hen is brown. It feeds on insects, earthworms, fruit and seeds, and has a beautiful song.

▲Tree sparrow 13–14cm
Sometimes seen in parks and gardens. It is smaller than the house sparrow, has a black spot on each cheek, a smaller black bib, and the crown of its head is chestnut.

▲ Great tit 14cm
This common garden bird is larger than the blue tit. It is often seen looking for seeds or insects in low bushes or on the ground.

▲Jackdaw 33cm
This bird lives in colonies near old buildings, such as churches, or in parks with old trees. It eats mainly insects, seeds, eggs and young birds.

◄Pied wagtail 18cm
This perky bird can be seen chasing winged insects in parks and even on quite busy roads. It nests in a bank or wall. The female's back is grey.

▲Starling 21–22cm
Thousands of these noisy birds roost on large buildings in town centres, and in the trees of town squares. Many may fly to the country to feed each day and return at night.

▼ Greenfinch 14.5cm
This finch is now commoner in towns than it is in the country. It often nests in garden shrubs, and feeds mainly on seeds and tree-buds.

▼ Bullfinch 15cm
A bird of the suburbs, with a short, sharp, strong bill. In spring it often eats buds from fruit trees, destroying the crop before it has formed.

▲ Robin 14cm
This woodland bird is often seen in gardens, picking up worms and insects from newly-dug soil. It also eats seeds and fruit. The male is very aggressive.

▲ Chaffinch 15cm
This common finch can be seen in suburban gardens and parks. It is a seed-eater and will visit the bird table in winter. The young are fed on insects.

▲ Goldfinch 12cm
This acrobatic and attractive little bird can sometimes be seen in groups on derelict land and rubbish tips. It eats mainly thistle seeds.

▲ Tawny owl 38cm
A large bird with a quavering 'hoo-hoo' call. It rests in old trees during the day. At night it hunts mice, voles and other small animals.

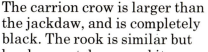

▲ Carrion crow 47cm
The carrion crow is larger than the jackdaw, and is completely black. The rook is similar but has bare patches round its beak.

Beaks

There is a close link between the shape of a bird's beak and the type of food that it eats.

1 The mallard's flat beak is used to skim food, such as plants, from the water.

2 With its hooked beak the kestrel tears the flesh of the animals it eats.

3 The swallow's fine beak can open wide to seize insects as it flies.

5 The pigeon's beak enables it to pick up quite large seeds and scraps.

4 The strong beak of the greenfinch can crack quite large seeds.

6 The wren has a long fine beak, with which it probes for insects in tree bark.

Inside a house

People share their houses with many other animals and plants. Some are welcome. Pets and house plants are brought into the home deliberately. Some animals, like the silverfish and firebrat, move in almost unnoticed. Others, including fleas, bugs and lice, are pests.

All thrive on the extra warmth and shelter provided by the house and its inhabitants.

▼ Uninvited plants

Most unwanted plants are harmless, though in time they may damage brickwork. **Lichens** like the ones below often grow on the roofs of old houses. There are many different species, varying in shape and colour. Each is two plants, a fungus living with an alga.

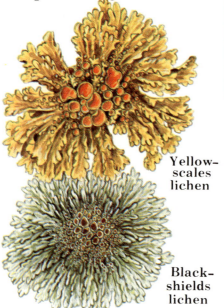

Yellow-scales lichen

Black-shields lichen

Liverworts may grow on damp walls, such as behind leaking drainpipes. They are usually flat green plants with curled leaves.

One plant is very unwelcome. **Dry rot fungus** (4) lives on old wood. If it gets into floorboards or roof supports it can seriously damage them.

Key
1 Mealy bug
2 Whitefly
3 Silverfish
4 Dry rot fungus
5 Brown rat
6 House spider
7 House mouse and nest
8 Ant
9 Flour beetle, cockroach, etc.
10 Cat flea

▲ Kitchen visitors

The kitchen is the most popular part of the house for many animals. Food is usually plentiful, and it is warm. Grain weevils and flour beetles (9) attack dry food. Cockroaches (9) feed on almost any food scraps. Ants (8) carry food away to their nests. Silverfish (3) and firebrats scavenge for crumbs of food.

Adult moth

Larva

▲**Case-bearing clothes moth**
There are several species of
clothes moth. The larva of this
one spins a 'case' in which it
lives. Like all moths, clothes
moths have larvae. They eat the
dirt in wool, hair and fur,
damaging clothes in particular.

Adult
beetle

Adult flea

Mealy bugs

Whitefly

Larva

Larva

Eggs

Larva

▲**Parasites on pets**
Some animals are parasites on
other house-dwellers. Domestic
cats and dogs are hosts to fleas
(above), which feed on their
blood. They have hard, flat
bodies which slide easily through
fur, and they can jump enormous
distances.

▲**Parasites on plants**
Plants which are brought into
the house may be attacked by
insects. The mealy bug (above
left) sucks plant sap.
   Whiteflies (above right) are
tiny two-winged insects, which
look like minute moths. They
weaken plants.

▲**Furniture beetle**
Furniture beetle larvae are
called **woodworms**. They
burrow into wood and live in
tunnels, eating the wood as they
go. Small round holes in
furniture and small piles of
sawdust on the floor show that
woodworms are at work.

Who lives in your house?

No matter how clean it is, any house has uninvited inhabitants.

*Not to scale. Adult body-length given.

▲**House cricket** 20mm
This cricket lives in old houses, where it is active at night, scavenging for food scraps. It is less common than it was, but can still be found outdoors in the warmth of rubbish tips.

▲**Common cockroach** 20–30mm
This insect feeds on food scraps at night. It thrives in dirty buildings, particularly dirty restaurants, and on waste tips, from which it carries diseases.

▲**Cellar spider** 8–10mm
This spider spins a web near the ceiling and can often be seen hanging upside down in the corner of a room. The female holds the egg cocoon in her jaws until the tiny spiders hatch.

▲**House spider** 11–14mm
This large brown spider is the one which often falls into the bath. It spins a large, matted sheet web which is rolled up to form a tunnel in one corner. It feeds on flies trapped in its web.

▲**Clothes moth** 11–15mm
This common moth can be found in summer. Its larvae feed mainly on dirty woollen clothes, making holes in them. They also attack fur and feathers, but not synthetic materials.

▲**Bluebottle** 8–11mm
A large, hairy, blue-bodied fly, whose wings make a buzzing sound. The one found in houses is usually the female, which comes indoors searching for meat on which to lay its eggs. It carries disease.

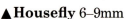

▲**Housefly** 6–9mm
This greyish fly is very common in houses. The adults lay their eggs on decaying matter or excrement, where the larvae hatch and develop. Flies carry diseases.

▲**Brown house moth** 20–23mm
This nocturnal moth enters houses in summer to lay its eggs. The larvae feed on scraps of animal or vegetable matter between floorboards and often damage carpets as well.

▲Silverfish 10mm
This small, wingless insect is common in houses, particularly in kitchens and bathrooms. It is active at night and will run for shelter when lights are switched on. It feeds on tiny scraps of food or wallpaper paste.

▲Firebrat 12mm
Like the silverfish, this is a bristletail, a type of wingless insect. It feeds on tiny food scraps, and needs warm surroundings in order to survive. This means that it is often only found near fireplaces or stoves.

▲Headlouse 1–3mm
This small louse is a parasite. It lives on humans, among hairs on the head. It pierces the skin and sucks blood. The white eggs (nits) are usually attached to hair or clothes. Headlice spread diseases.

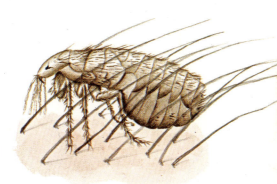

▲Black ant 4–9mm
Although it nests in gardens, the black ant often enters houses searching for food. It carries sugar and other loose foods back to its nest.

▲Bedbug 5–6mm
This bug is less common than it was. By day it hides in cracks between floor-boards or behind skirting boards. At night it sucks blood from sleeping people.

▲Flea 2-4mm
This irritating parasite sucks human blood, leaving an itchy bump. It can only live in dirty conditions, and is less common than it was.

▲Woodworm 4–5mm
This is a furniture beetle. The larva bores into wood, leaving small round holes and piles of dust. It can be introduced into a house in old second-hand furniture. The adults fly at night.

Life cycles

Insects have two different types of life cycle.
A The egg hatches into a larva, which turns into a pupa, then an adult. All look different.

B The egg hatches into a nymph, like a small, wingless adult. There may be several nymphs before the adult appears.

1 Egg | 2 Larva | 3 Pupa | 4 Adult

▲ A The life cycle of a housefly

▼ B The life cycle of a grasshopper

1 Egg | 2 Nymph | 3 Nymph | 4 Adult

More room for wildlife

Wildlife everywhere
As we have seen, animals and plants survive in towns and cities wherever they are given a chance. They will move into the most unlikely places and thrive there. Plants cover the ugliness of neglected sites with their leaves and flowers, and birds brighten morning and evening with their song.

Most people who live in towns are happy to share them with this variety of plants and animals. However, we can do a lot more than just accept that there will always be wildlife around us. We can make our towns more attractive to wildlife. They will become more attractive to people at the same time.

Planning for wildlife
New towns are being built all the time. They can be planned with parks and open spaces, lakes and streams, tree-lined streets and squares. These all make towns more pleasant for people and encourage many different animals and plants to live there.

It is harder to plan for wildlife in older towns, which often have very little green open space. However, many of the older buildings in towns are now being replaced by new houses and flats. These often include small parks and open spaces. Unfortunately, builders usually cover these with grass, which is then kept neatly trimmed. This may look tidy, but more imaginative planting could make these new green areas into important wildlife habitats. They would also be more beautiful to look at and walk in.

▲ **Trees are very important. Old trees may become diseased and have to be cut down, but too often healthy trees are felled unnecessarily.**

When old houses are demolished their gardens are often cleared. This can destroy important habitats, particularly if large trees are cut down. They take years to grow, and provide food and shelter for many different animals. If the new buildings are carefully planned old trees can be included.

Improving wasteland
After old houses have been demolished plants and animals move on to the derelict land. They can be encouraged in several ways.

First, large bits of rubble should be removed, or piled up and covered with earth. Some could be used to make paths and seats. If there are any large hollows left in the ground they could be lined with plastic sheeting to make ponds. These are very important, and will attract a wide variety of animal life. Insects such as dragonflies may come to breed in ponds, birds will bathe and drink in them, and you may even find toads, frogs and newts there.

Many plants will grow from seeds which are already in the earth or are blown in by the wind. You could also collect and scatter seeds from wasteland plants, or from your garden. Butterflies will be attracted by buddleia, a quick-growing, sweet-scented shrub.

Grow as many different plants as possible, so that different species of insects and birds come to live and feed on the site. All the bare earth should be covered after only a year's growth. A fascinating new habitat will exist for you and the animals to enjoy – until the builders arrive.

Grow plants yourself
The smallest green open space in a town is probably a window box. If you have a window, you can have a window box. It should be properly made, with broken pots at the bottom to help drainage, and good compost on top. Window boxes usually need watering very often, since they dry out quickly. A few sweet-scented, nectar-producing flowers will provide food for many different insects.

A balcony will hold larger plants, which flower for longer and feed more animals.

▲ **Digging a hole for a garden pond. Birds will drink and bathe there, and dragonflies may come to breed and catch insects.**

Gardens

Gardens are probably the most important habitats in towns. They can be improved in several easy ways so that more animals can live there.

The first step is to avoid killing animals whenever possible. Chemical insecticides are very useful because they kill pests, such as aphids and other insects which damage plants. But they also kill harmless insects, and mean that there is far less food for larger animals, such as birds, which eat insects. They should therefore be used very carefully, and only when really necessary.

Flowers attract thousands of insects in a summer. Some are food plants for bees, others for butterflies and moths. Plants such as hollyhocks and foxgloves, Michaelmas daisies and phlox, will feed many different insects and birds.

In a large garden, one corner can be set aside for wild plants, like nettles, brambles, thistles and coarse grass. Butterfly caterpillars feed on them. To encourage moth caterpillars, you should plant willow, willowherb, privet and other small shrubs.

Attracting birds

Where there are insects, birds will follow. They need shrubs in which to hunt and shelter, and trees as look-out posts and night-time roosts. It is usually a mistake to plant trees like oak, ash and beech in city gardens. They grow too tall and cut out most of the light, and their roots can damage the foundations of the house.

Choose smaller trees such as rowan, silver birch, holly whitebeam, guelder rose and willow. Decorative introduced trees like maples, laburnum, lilac and Japanese cherries all give shelter.

If you are lucky, blackbirds, thrushes, hedge sparrows and wrens may nest in your garden. You can encourage hole-nesting birds, like the blue tit and great tit, with nestboxes.

▲ **As old trees die, new ones should be planted to replace them. The holes dug should be large enough to let the roots be spread out.**

One of the most valuable features which can be added to a garden is water. Natural ponds are disappearing rapidly from the countryside, and with them go many plants and animals. A ready-made garden pond can be put into a hollow, or a larger hole can be dug and lined with plastic sheeting.

If a few plants are added at the edge and underwater, they will quickly take root and the pond will rapidly become full of animal life. Garden ponds could become the most important habitats for frogs, toads and newts, as countryside ponds are destroyed. If these animals do come to your pond, don't put goldfish in it, because these fish may eat their eggs.

Parks

Parks are larger versions of gardens, and can be improved in the same ways. More can be done in a park, however, because it is larger. This is the best place to grow large native trees, such as oak, ash and beech.

Most parks are very well-kept. The grass is mown, flower beds are regularly dug and replanted, and hedges are trimmed. A slightly wilder park is more attractive to plants and animals, and therefore to many visitors. For example, far more insects live in long rough grass than on a well-mown lawn.

Some parks are designed to copy the countryside. They are called landscape gardens or ecological parks. Soil and plants may be brought from different habitats in the surrounding countryside, so that the park is made up of different miniature habitats.

Pinewoods give way to heathland and bog, oak woods and meadows mix with ponds and streams, each with its own plants and animals. People in towns can learn much about the surrounding countryside from these landscape gardens.

It is very easy to destroy town habitats, and many of them only last for a short time before the land is built on. These are just a few of the ways in which new habitats can be created, all helping to improve towns and cities as places for plants, animals (and people) to live in.

▲ **A fairly wild corner of a garden. It is bright with sweet-scented flowers which will attract bees and other insects.**

Word list

Annual A plant that grows from seed, flowers, produces seed and dies in one year.

Antenna Fine sense organ on the head of an insect.

Aquatic Living in water.

Broadleaved A tree which has leaves shaped like flat blades.

Carnivore Flesh-eating animal or plant.

Colonization The process by which animals and plants move into a new habitat.

Competition The struggle between two or more plants or animals to occupy a particular living space.

Conifer A tree whose fruits are cones. These trees usually have needle-shaped leaves.

Conservation The science of managing and protecting natural resources, including plants and animals.

Deciduous A tree which loses its leaves in winter.

Diurnal Active by day.

Dormant Resting. Many plants pass the winter in a dormant state.

Ecology The study of the relationship between animals, plants and their environment.

Ecosystem A group of animals and plants with their non-living environment.

Evergreen A tree which does not lose its leaves in winter.

Habitat The environment in which an animal or plant lives.

Hibernation Passing the winter in a deep sleep.

Incubation Sitting on eggs until they hatch. Used of birds.

Insectivore A bird or mammal which eats mainly insects.

Invertebrate An animal without a backbone.

Larva An immature stage in an insect life-cycle, between egg and pupa. It looks completely different to the adult.

Metamorphosis Change of shape in insect life history e.g. egg to larva to pupa to adult or egg to nymph to adult.

Micro-habitat A small part of a habitat, e.g. a dead tree is a micro-habitat in the park habitat.

Migration The movement of animals to a new habitat. Usually seasonal. Caused by changes in weather, food supply, etc.

Niche The place which a particular animal or plant occupies in an ecosystem.

Nocturnal Active at night.

Nymph Immature stage in the life history of an insect which does not pupate. Resembles the adult in many ways, but usually has no wings.

Organism General term for any living thing.

Parasite An animal or plant which feeds on another animal or plant, called the host, without killing it.

Perennial A plant that lives for several years.

Predator An animal which kills other animals for food.

Proboscis Tube-shaped mouth-parts of an insect, used for sucking up liquid food.

Pupa Stage in insect life history during which the larva changes into its adult form.

Resident An animal which lives in one country or region throughout the year.

Succession Development in a plant community whereby one group of plants is gradually replaced by another.

Terrestrial Living on land.

Territory An area of land or water which is defended by one animal against other members of the same species.

Vertebrate An animal with a backbone.

How to find out more

Books

There are hundreds of books about European wildlife. Those listed here are only a very small selection. Visit your local **bookshops** and **libraries** to find what else is available.

If you are not already a member of the local library, it would be an excellent idea for you to join. Although you will probably want to own some of the books on this list, many will be used for occasional reference only and can be seen in your library.

These books will all give you more information on some aspects of **urban wildlife**:
London's Natural History R. Fitter (Collins);
The Naturalist in London M. Burton (David & Charles);
The Ecology of Towns A. Leutscher (Franklin Watts);
The Unofficial Countryside R. Mabey (Collins);
Animals in the Garden H. Angel (Jarrold);
Towns and Gardens D. Owen (Hodder & Stoughton);
Nature in Towns D. Gilman (Macdonald New Reference Library).

You may be interested in doing some **practical project work**. The following books contain suggestions for practical work:
Wildlife Conservation by Young People R. Arnold (Ward Lock Educational);
The Family Naturalist M. Chinery (Macdonald and Jane);
Wildlife Areas for Schools (Durham County Conservation Trust);
Parks and Open Spaces R. Purton (Blandford Press);
City Wildlife (RSPCA).

One of the main problems for anyone who is starting to study wildlife, either in towns or in the country, is the **identification** of the plants and animals which are seen. To help the beginner, many publishers have produced whole series of books devoted to the identification of different groups of animals and plants. New books appear all the time. Keep your eyes open for the series which you find most useful.

Remember, you will not be able to identify correctly everything that you see. Do not be discouraged. You will soon learn to recognize the most common plants and animals of the area where you live. Practice makes perfect. These are some of the most popular series and books.

The Observer Book of ... series (Warne) Small pocket books on almost every topic. Useful for identification of common species and containing simple information on each subject.
Wayside and Woodland series (Warne) Much more detailed than the Observer series, and more expensive. Good colour plates. Separate titles on butterflies, moths, beetles, flies, etc.
Field Guide series (Collins) An excellent collection of guides giving details of origin, distribution, variation.
The Oxford Book of ... series (Oxford University Press) Attractive books, designed for the beginner. Well illustrated.
The Young Specialist looks at ... (Burke) A series illustrated by clear line drawings and photographs. Good, concise information.
Colour Identification Guide to British Butterflies T. G. Howarth (Warne) Superb photographs.

Organizations

Knowledge does not only come from books. You can learn more about urban wildlife in many different ways. There are always people more expert than you who will be happy to help you to learn. You may be able to join a local or national **club** or **society** where you will meet people with similar interests to your own. Many societies organize field trips or conservation activities.

Make use of the services offered by your local **museum**. Many local museums have natural history collections. They are also often the places where records about local plants and animals are kept. The curator of the museum will be able to help with the identification of specimens, or will tell you who to take them to. Many museums also have children's clubs.

Join a local **Natural History Society** or **County Naturalists' Trust**. You can find the address in your local library or community centre. These clubs arrange lectures, film shows and quizzes and are an excellent way of making friends with local naturalists. In summer, they also usually arrange a series of field trips. County Naturalists' Trusts usually own one or more nature reserves which provide an opportunity for people to become involved in practical conservation work.

Find out about your local **parks**. They may be much more interesting than you think. Many Parks Departments have set up nature trails in their parks. Why not write to the Parks Department of your own local council to find out if there are any nature trails near to your own home? You will find the address in the telephone directory.

If you are particularly interested in **conservation**, you may like to join one of the youth groups run by the **World Wildlife Fund**. The groups and activities vary according to the age of members. For details, write to the World Wildlife Fund, 29 Greville Street, London EC1N 8AX.

The **Royal Society for the Protection of Birds (RSPB)** has a junior section called the **Young Ornithologists' Club (YOC)**. It publishes a magazine and arranges projects, competitions and activities. For details, write to:
Young Ornithologists' Club,
The Lodge,
Sandy,
Bedfordshire.

Always enclose a stamped addressed envelope when asking for information.

If there is a **zoo** near you, see if they have a junior membership scheme. Many zoos are now very interested in conservation and are taking a lot of trouble to breed animals which are threatened with extinction. There may well be a junior membership scheme with a magazine, film shows and other activities.

Things to do

You do not always have to wait for other people to help you to learn more about city wildlife. There are many things that you can do on your own, or with friends who have similar interests.

Make a garden nature reserve

You will need to talk to your parents before you start on this project. They would not understand if you started planting 'weeds' in part of the garden which they have just weeded! Indeed, they may not approve of everything that you want to do in order to make your garden a better place for wildlife. You could suggest one or two of the following.

Plant one or two native **trees** in your garden.

Build a **bird table** to feed the birds in winter.

Make and put up a few **nestboxes**. You can buy plans for a variety of nestboxes from the British Trust for Ornithology, Beech Grove, Tring, Herts HP3 5NR.

Plant **shrubs** and **flowers** which attract insects. Buddleia is cheap, grows easily and is attractive to many different insects.

Allow one corner of the garden to go **wild**. Encourage nettles and other plants that are the food of butterflies and moths.

Build a **pond**. Stock the pond with a few native water plants, insects and fish. If you can persuade frogs, toads or newts to live in the pond and garden, this will be particularly valuable.

Grow a mixed **shrubbery** to give shelter for insects and to produce winter berries as food for local birds.

Try not to use **chemical sprays**. This will reduce the destruction of honey bees and other useful insects.

Start a school Natural History Society

Get together with a few of your friends and try to persuade one or two of your teachers to start the society with you. You could form a school group of the Wildlife Youth Service (details from the World Wildlife Fund – address above). Or you could get help from the local Natural History Society, who can suggest speakers, activities, etc.

One very ambitious project for a school Natural History Society is to establish a **school Nature Reserve**. This will involve many of the activities listed under 'Make a garden nature reserve'. You can also be more ambitious. If the reserve is tucked away in a corner, you can encourage more of the plants which we normally call weeds. Your teachers may also be able to get advice from the Information Service, Nature Conservancy Council, Calthorpe House, Calthorpe Street, Banbury, Oxon OX16 8EX.

The school society can also play a part in the general conservation of city wildlife. Litter can be dangerous. Why not organize a **litter clearance campaign** at a local open space?

Write to the **local council** to find out how interested the council is in local wildlife conservation. Letters could ask, for example, how many trees the council has planted in the past year. If you can establish a close link with the local council, then you can learn a great deal – and so can they!

Turn a derelict site into an ecological park

This is a project for the *very* enthusiastic! Help from parents, teachers and other interested adults will be essential. First of all, find your site. Ask the council if they have any derelict sites that will be lying idle for a few years.

Once you have the site, you can begin to plan your park, trying to create copies of natural habitats. Will they be grass, woodland, water or something else? What soil is needed? Where will the plants come from? The whole business is complex, but very exciting. Expert advice can be obtained from the Ecological Parks Trust, c/o The Linnean Society, Burlington House, Piccadilly, London W1V 0LQ.

Index